ROASTING, BREWING AND MORE

How To Enjoy Coffee Beyond Your Morning Routine

STELLA PERRY

CONTENTS

INTRODUCTION **07**

HISTORY AND ORIGINS OF COFFEE **11**
   History 12
   Geographical Origins and Spread 12

THE COFFEE MAKING PROCESS **15**
   How it's Grown 16
   How it's Harvested 18
   How it's Processed 19

THE COFFEE TRADE **21**
   Traditional Coffee Consumerism 23
   Fair Trade Coffee 25
   Environmental Concerns and Practices 26

HOW COFFEE IS ROASTED **31**
   What is Coffee Roasting? 32
   Types of Heat Used in Coffee Roasting 33
   How to Tell if Coffee has Finished Roasting 34
   Purchasing a Roaster 36
   How to Roast Raw Coffee Beans in a Roaster 37
   Roasting Safety 37
   Tips and Tricks During and After Roasting 38

ROASTING COFFEE AT HOME **41**
   Where to Buy Green Coffee Beans 42
   Items You'll Need 44
   Oven Roasting 45
   Popcorn Popper 47
   Cooling and Waiting 49

HOW TO BUY AND STORE COFFEE **51**
   Whole Bean vs. Ground 52
   Whole coffee beans 53
   Ground coffee beans 53
   Roasting Date 54
   Roaster Information 56
   Origin 57
   Storage Options 58

HOW TO TASTE COFFEE **61**
   Breathe it In 62
   Sip Slowly 63
   Take a Drink 65
   Consider the Flavor Palate 66

GRINDING COFFEE SUCCESSFULLY 69

Choose the Right Grinder 71
Standard Burr Grinder 71
Bladed Grinder 71
Conical Burr Grinder...72
Hand Crank Grinder 72
Choose the Right Grind Level..72
Grinding Coffee Without a Grinder 75

METHODS OF BREWING 77

Drip Filters 78
French Press..79
Pour Over..80
Turkish Coffee 81
Espresso Machine 82
Percolator and Cowboy Coffee.. 83

CHOOSING THE RIGHT WATER FOR BREWING....................85

Soft vs. Hard Water...86
Filtered Tap Water...87
Bottled Water..88
Reverse Osmosis Water..88

EXPERIENCE ESPRESSO: NOT ALL BEANS ARE THE SAME.............91

How is Espresso Different from Coffee? 92
How to Brew Espresso..96

COMBINING ESPRESSO AND MILK..................................... 99

Lattes..100
Cappuccinos 102
Macchiatos..103

HOW TO MAKE LATTE ART 107

What You Need..108
Easy Designs to Try at Home 109
Helpful Hints..110

EXPANDING YOUR HORIZONS 113

Coffee-Based Drinks...114
Coffee-Based Desserts...116

CONCLUSION 121

INTRODUCTION

Have you ever wanted to learn more about coffee or expand your coffee horizons a little more? If so, you've come to the right place. Whether you're a coffee aficionado or you're just getting started in the world of enjoying your morning brew, we've got all the information you need to learn about coffee from bean to cup—and beyond.

WHAT IS COFFEE?

The word "coffee" can either refer to the coffee plant, the coffee bean, or the drink that is made from this bean. However, most of the time, this term refers to the drink.

Coffee is made by first harvesting the beans of the coffee plant. From there, the beans are dried, processed, and roasted to the perfect temperature to create different roasting strengths and flavors. These beans are then brewed along with hot water to create the beverage that we all know and love.

There's a lot more to coffee than simply that cup you reach for every morning. In this book, you'll learn everything you've ever wanted to know about where coffee comes from, how it's made, and what you can do with the beans once you buy them.

So let's get started!

REVIEWS

FREE BONUS:
10 FREE RECIPES FOR DELICIOUS COFFEE DRINKS YOU CAN MAKE AT HOME

GO TO HTTP://TINYURL.COM/Y5X5T4FN
TO DOWNLOAD YOUR FREE RECIPE BOOK

DOWNLOAD THE AUDIO VERSION OF THIS BOOK FREE!

IF YOU LOVE LISTENING TO AUDIOBOOKS ON-THE-GO OR ENJOY THE NARRATION AS YOU READ ALONG, I HAVE GREAT NEWS FOR YOU. YOU CAN DOWNLOAD THE AUDIO BOOK VERSION OF ROASTING, BREWING AND MORE FOR FREE JUST BY SIGNING UP FOR A FREE 30-DAY AUDIBLE TRIAL. JUST SCAN OR USE THE LINKS BELOW:

HTTPS://TINYURL.COM/Y5QAKCC4
FOR AUDIBLE US

HTTPS://TINYURL.COM/YXTPD3WJ
FOR AUDIBLE UK

HISTORY AND ORIGINS OF COFFEE

Coffee has been around for a long time. In fact, it dates back all the way to

the 1400s, and may have even been around earlier than this. In this chapter, we'll take a very brief look at the history and origins of this classic drink.

HISTORY

Many scholars believe that coffee has existed for much longer than written record shows, and it's thought to have had its origins in Ethiopia. Early written documentation also points to Yemen as one of the first locations where coffee was introduced, although it didn't take long for it to make its way throughout the Middle East and onward. As explorers from Europe began traveling to the Middle East, they were introduced to coffee and brought it back to their own shores as well.

Even in its early days, coffee was consumed in coffee houses as well as in private residences. In this way, coffee has always been at the center of social experiences. Unfortunately, this also caused some religious leaders to believe the drink was satanic, leading to several bans on coffee in different parts of the world.

GEOGRAPHICAL ORIGINS AND SPREAD

Although there's no way to know for sure when coffee was first used as a drink, many myths surrounding this beverage claim that it was discovered by a Sufi (Islamic mystic). According to legend, he witnessed birds with an excess of energy, and decided to try eating the beans they had been consuming to get the same energy for himself. From there, the first understanding of coffee and its properties was born.

Coffee's popularity eventually spread to Egypt and throughout the Middle East, and it soon took off in India, Persia, and Africa too. For a long while, it was largely related to religious practices, particularly in Islamic nations. Soon after, it became popularized in Italy, Asia, and the Americas as well. Despite its ban for some time by the Catholic church, it nevertheless hung on and eventually became the widespread and beloved drink that it is today.

"Coffee has always been at the center of social experiences ever since it was first enjoyed."

THE COFFEE MAKING PROCESS

The coffee making process

begins with farmers who grow the beans, it's more complicated than that. It takes a professional to know and understand coffee plants well enough to make a living from their production. However, even the casual coffee consumer can benefit from a little extra understanding of what it takes to grow and harvest coffee before it's sold to importers or exporters. In this chapter, we'll take a quick look at how coffee is grown, harvested, and processed in order to get it ready to sell and eventually make its way to the shelves of markets and cafes around the world.

HOW IT'S GROWN

There are two different types of coffee plants, which actually grow on shrubs or trees, although one is much more commonly recognized and widely used than the other. *Coffea robusta* is the lesser-known of the two. It is most commonly grown and used in Africa and Vietnam, and it has a much more bitter and rich flavor than the other type of coffee. Although only about 30% of the coffee sold and consumed worldwide comes from the robusta plant, some countries are starting to catch on to its unique flavor. In some instances, both types of beans are brewed together to provide a twist on the classics.

The other type of coffee plant is *Coffea arabica*, which is much more widespread. If you look at just about any bag of coffee beans, you're likely to see the word "arabica," as this is the type of plant your beans probably come from. Arabica beans account for 70% of coffee sold worldwide, and they have a much milder flavor than that of the robusta plant. When discussing coffee roasting, brewing, and tasting throughout this book, we will be referring to the arabica bean unless otherwise specified.

Coffee grows in an area called the bean belt, which has the perfect (more tropical) climate for growing these plants. The plants cannot grow nearly as well in other parts of the world, so their production is fairly limited. The plants were traditionally cultivated in the shade beneath taller trees to encourage them to grow as healthy and as large as possible, and to increase the production of coffee beans per plant. However, as the demand for coffee has increased around the world, sun tolerant plants have emerged. A significant characteristic of coffee beans from sun tolerant plants is that sunlight reduces the incidence of fungal disease which can beset the plant and reduce crop yield.

Coffee beans are initially green when they first appear. If left unpicked, they will eventually turn yellow and then red. They are most commonly picked after they have turned a deep shade of red. Typically it takes two to three years for a given coffee plant to grow beans.

19

HOW IT'S HARVESTED

Harvesting coffee is a labor-intensive job that takes a lot of work and effort to accomplish. The harvesting stage itself accounts for most of the overall coffee making process. When the beans first come in green, they are latter picked by hand when they are ripe. This is a very time-consuming task, since the coffee shrubs are so large that finding all the beans on a given plant can be tricky. It is uncommon, however, for coffee beans to be harvested by machine, since doing so can severely harm the plants themselves and can also damage to the surrounding rainforests. Because coffee growing areas are often mountainous, only in very flat locations can beans be harvested by machine.

Coffee beans are usually harvested once per year, although this can vary depending on the location and the size of the farm in question. In some parts of the world, the climate is so conducive to coffee growing that plants will bear fruit twice per year instead of just once, such as Colombia, Ethiopia and Kenya.

When coffee is harvested by machine, it's usually done by strip picking. This process strips the fruit of the coffee bush from its branches all at the same time. When hand picking occurs, however, the beans are only picked when they are ripe beans, so the selection process can be more customized. In handpicking situations, pickers are assigned a specific plant to work on for a few days, and then they rotate to a different plant. This gives the beans on each plant a chance to ripen and be harvested at the right time, and it also makes it easier for all of the beans to be examined for readiness.

Once the picking day has ended, the individual picker's product for the day is weighed before being sent off to be processed. A skilled picker can pick between 100-200 pounds of coffee a day, which results in 20-40 pounds of roasted coffee beans.

HOW IT'S PROCESSED

Since coffee beans begin to spoil once they've been removed from the plants, it's important to start processing them right away after they've been harvested. The most common coffee processing technique is called the dry method, in which batches of harvested beans are allowed to dry by being spread out on a tarp in the sun. While the sun is up, the beans are turned, raked and stirred to allow them all to dry evenly and to prevent any rotting that may otherwise occur. Once the sun goes down, they are covered up to prevent rain or moisture from reaching them.

An important reason for drying beans in the processing phase is to reduce the moisture inside the beans to 11%. Below this level coffee loses flavor, and above it, beans can mold. The dry method of coffee processing can sometimes take many weeks to complete, particularly if it's very wet or humid outside at the time.

The other type of coffee processing is known as the wet method. In this technique, the pulp from the inside of the coffee bean is removed after the beans are harvested. This is performed by a machine that separates the inner pulp from the outer skin. This process produces coffee pulp waste, but in many environmentally-friendly and sustainable coffee farming productions, the pulp is used as a natural fertilizer to help improve the coffee harvest for the next year.

After the bean pulp is removed, the beans are then sorted mechanically based on weight and then by size. From there, they go into containers filled with water, where they soak for a day or two to remove the outside layer of the skin. This effectively ferments the beans, leaving them with the perfect texture for final drying and finishing. This process is not possible in countries where there are frequent water shortages, so it is less common in some parts of the world.

No matter which method is used, the beans are then hulled by machine. They may be machine-polished at this stage as well. The final step is to sort them by weight and size once again, and to throw out any beans that have noticeable flaws. This is usually performed by hand, but it may also be completed by a machine. This decision depends on the specific farm or producer. When the entire process is complete, the end result is green coffee that is ready to be roasted.

THE COFFEE TRADE

It's no secret

that coffee is one of the most popular drinks in the world. People around the world love it, and have for a very long time. Because of this, coffee is a vastly important commodity, second only to crude oil. When learning all about coffee, it's important to understand all aspects of this trade, and necessary to acknowledge that there are also favorable and unfavorable elements. In this chapter, we'll break down the coffee trade into simple but thorough sections to help make it easier to see just where your coffee comes from.

TRADITIONAL COFFEE CONSUMERISM

Coffee is made by small companies, farmers, and producers who make up the vast majority of suppliers around the world. These exist largely throughout South America, but they can be found elsewhere too. The coffee growing process is very strenuous and requires a great deal of labor to accomplish. Even so, coffee is regularly traded worldwide and is a valuable commodity, typically produced by developing countries.

World events can lead to the rise and fall of the cost of coffee. When wars and other events occur and impact trade, the price of coffee goes up. Embargos and new trade agreements with developing countries may also affect the price of coffee and lead to price changes. In 1986, when Vietnam began exporting coffee to the United States, it heavily affected the Brazilian coffee industry, which led to some Brazilian farmers giving up their jobs and cutting ties with the coffee-making trade. Of course, this also led to a supply and demand issue that further caused the price of beans to fluctuate.

Local cafés, as well as coffee chains like Starbucks, also affect the price of beans. These stores are able to sell coffee and coffee-based beverages for much higher than the cost of their ingredients and in turn, they pay different prices for the coffee beans they use. Some of these chains and local cafés are committed to buying fair trade coffee, which we will discuss in depth below. However, some are not, and they further affect an already unpredictable market.

As China and Russia began to drink more coffee per year in 2016 and 2017, the price of coffee beans rose once again, and this increase in price is still going on today. This also affects the price of coffee stocks, which can be bought and sold the same as any other type of stock.

The chain of coffee trade starts with the producers (farmers and plantations) that grow and harvest the coffee beans, and then goes to the exporters and importers who handle moving that coffee from one country to another. These exporters and importers have most of the control over the types of coffee varieties that are eventually sold to customers around the world. For example, if the importers have a unique type of coffee bean available but are charging exorbitant prices for it, roasters will be unable to buy it, and so it likely won't see widespread use.

Once it is imported, coffee is then picked up by roasters who process it into a form that can be brewed. Roasters pay wholesale prices from importers for their beans and then mark up the price when they sell the beans to retailers such as coffee companies, markets, and cafés. Because of this, the roasters tend to make the most money out of the whole coffee trade process.

Only after the beans reach the retailers do they finally come to you, the consumer. Coffee has a long journey from bean to cup, and it's not always an easy one. However, it is an interesting one, and it can be beneficial to take some time to stop and think about where your coffee has come from the next time you buy a bag of beans.

> # *Coffee has a long journey from bean to cup, and it's not always an easy one.*

FAIR TRADE COFFEE

There are many concerns associated with the production and sales of coffee beans around the world from start to finish. As previously mentioned, many coffee farmers in Brazil and other South American countries have been forced to give up their farms and move into sometimes unpleasant and unsafe conditions because they have been unable to sell their product at a profit for a long time. This issue led to a worldwide focus on fair trade coffee, which is still widely recognized today.

The World Fair Trade Organization defines fair trade as a partnership stating that true fair trading must include "dialogue, transparency and respect," and that it must improve conditions for workers who are negatively impacted by the state of trade and its common practices. Organizations that focus on fair trade products work to encourage positive changes in the climate of the coffee trade while still keeping consumers happy. Fair trade certification can be applied to other products, but coffee is one of the most well-known. Fair trade certification can be applied to other products, but coffee is one of the most well-known, and is also one of the products that made this term well-known.

Fair trade allows the producer of the coffee to communicate with importers and negotiate for his or her own benefit . Producers are paid a flat rate for their coffee beans and in turn, importers and exporters then help them reduce their debt so they can continue to farm their product.

In order to be certified as fair trade, a farm must meet certain regulations. However, this isn't the only step required, and some farms that meet these requirements still cannot be certified as fair trade because they can't afford the high cost of getting the certification. For this reason, there are some people who feel fair trade is not beneficial in the long run, and that it really only helps larger corporations that don't do much to assist smaller farmers.

ENVIRONMENTAL CONCERNS AND PRACTICES

There are many environmental issues and concerns related to the production of coffee. As coffee consumers become more environmentally-minded, these concerns have increasingly come to light. While not all consumers stop to think about the environmental impact of their coffee purchases, many do, and it's important to understand what those impacts may be before making a purchase.

Coffee farms and South American coffee plantations have historically provided a safe and secluded habitat for many species of insects and birds that live within the shade of the coffee trees. These farms are similar to small forests and are important parts of the ecological systems in the countries where they are located. These farms are run using old-fashioned and traditional methods, utilizing waste from the coffee production process as fertilizer and handling pest control with no need for chemicals. They don't use fertilizers, and they also regularly grow banana trees which provide shade to help the coffee trees grow, and to provide food for themselves and their families.

This traditional method of coffee cultivation changed when the United States paid these countries and producers to upgrade their methods to more technologically advanced ones. While these new methods mean coffee can be produced more quickly, they also heavily damage forests as well as plant and animal life throughout the areas. Another serious concern is climate change, which, if it raises the average temperature in coffee-growing area, poses a significant threat to the coffee trade.

Replacing the natural shading of coffee and banana trees with different, modernized growing methods can destroy the habitats of many species of birds and insects that call coffee farms their

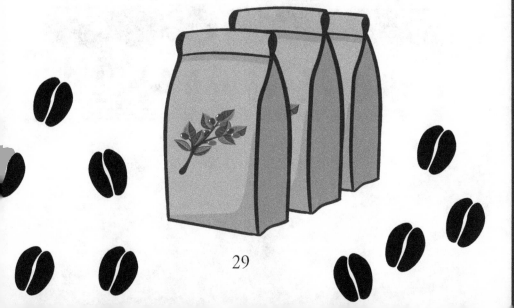

homes. In addition, the new methods that are used, including sun cultivation, require chemical fertilizers and pesticides in order to work properly. These chemicals contribute to a rise in pollution of the groundwater and surface water at or near coffee farms, and can also lead to further habitat destruction throughout Latin America. As these methods continue to be used, soil quality can diminish, and deforestation can spread rapidly.

This problem persists even today, although it has been widely recognized as an issue for some time. Only in recent years have local governments and others involved in the coffee trade sought to repair the damage caused by the modernization of coffee production. Today, some growers are offering higher prices for farming coffee via environmentally-sustainable practices. Other coffees are allowed to be certified as bird-friendly, organic, or shade-grown to show that they are grown using more eco-friendly methods of growing and harvesting. In the future, many coffee consumers, as well as organizations and corporations, hope to shift coffee farms back to their sustainable roots.

HOW COFFEE IS ROASTED

Although most people know that coffee beans are roasted

before they're sold to consumers, the process by which this happens is not necessarily common knowledge. Understanding your coffee from the ground up can help you better appreciate this beverage every time you take a sip, and learning about the process of coffee roasting can make a big difference in how you enjoy your morning brew. In this chapter, we'll discuss what coffee roasting is, as well as some of the specifics for anyone looking to get started using a roaster.

WHAT IS COFFEE ROASTING?

Coffee roasting is the process by which coffee is transformed from its natural state to one that can be used for brewing and drinking. When coffee beans first begin the roasting process, they are still green, but by the time they've finished roasting, they take on the distinct brown color. Roasting relies heavily on chemical processes that increase the flavor of the bean while somewhat decreasing the caffeine content.

Coffee roasting follows a step-by-step order that sounds simple, but relies on a highly skilled professional roaster to ensure it is handled appropriately to prevent unpleasant tastes in the finished product. First, the beans are sorted to remove any unfit individual beans, as well as any unwanted contaminants that may have made their way into the supply.

Next, the beans are weighed and then taken to the roaster, where they first absorb heat and then give off the heat themselves, cooking thoroughly to the perfect temperature. At the end of the process, the beans are cooled before moving along to the next phase on their journey to becoming coffee.

TYPES OF HEAT USED IN COFFEE ROASTING

There are two types of heat used in coffee roasting: endothermic and exothermic. Endothermic heat, means that the heat comes from an outside source and surrounds the coffee bean, warming it up and cooking it from the outside in. This step is required to begin the roasting process and to help the bean reach the right color and roasting level to achieve the flavor the roaster is looking for. This type of heat continues until the temperature in the roaster reaches about 175 degrees Celsius, or 347 degrees Fahrenheit.

Once this temperature is reached, the coffee beans are then switched to an exothermic cooking process. This means that the beans themselves give off the heat they have absorbed, which causes them to more or less roast each other. At this time, the roaster will likely be carefully monitoring the cooking process to ensure the beans don't get too hot or cool down too much to reach the right flavor and roasting level.

Both types of heat involved in coffee roasting represent a precise process that can easily be thrown off if the temperature ranges get too out of control. This is just one of the reasons why coffee roasting is such a difficult skill to master, and why it takes a lot of practice to learn.

HOW TO TELL IF COFFEE HAS FINISHED ROASTING

One of the most important steps in roasting coffee is determining when it's finished roasting. This takes a lot of practice, but it is possible to get the hang of it. Some very experienced roasters can sometimes tell just by looking at the bean when it's finished, but usually other methods are preferred in order to get a more precise roast.

Another way to tell that coffee is finished roasting is to smell it. Coffee beans will begin to smell like coffee as they roast, and the longer they go, the more coffee-like the aroma will become. Just remember that if they go too long, they'll smell burnt and will have an unpleasant flavor.

The final way to check whether or not your beans have finished roasting is to listen to them. When the roasting process begins, you'll hear a pop from the beans—known as the crack—much like you'd hear from popcorn. This initial pop means the beans have reached the very lightest stage of browning at which they can feasibly be brewed into coffee. However, you'll need to let them go much longer if you want them to reach other roasting levels. They will pop a second time when they've reached the realm of dark roast, so remember that medium roast coffee falls somewhere in between these two pops.

DIFFERENT LEVELS OF ROASTING

Technically, there are three levels of roasting. However, there are many different names and styles of roasts that fall into these three categories. Some of these individual styles differ from each other by just a few short minutes of roasting time, so it's important to be very careful when trying to get a specific taste out of your coffee beans. Keep these categories in mind to help you get a better idea of which roasting names fall into which levels:

» LIGHT ROAST. This category of roasting includes beans that look dry on the outside and have only popped once. They do not taste like roasted beans yet and have more acidity as well as a higher caffeine content than other roasts, since they are closer to their natural form.

Light roasts include New England roast, cinnamon roast, and moderate-light roast, among others.

» MEDIUM ROAST. This roasting category has popped once but has been roasted past that point. These beans are also dry on the outside and have a slightly more bitter, roasted flavor than light roasts, but not much. They are less acidic and fall in the middle in terms of caffeine content.

Medium roasts include City roast and Full City roast, among others.

» DARK ROAST. This type of roast causes the outside of the bean to become shiny and look oily. This is because the oils inside the beans have started rising to the surface. Dark roasted beans will pop twice before they're finished roasting, and they taste much more bitter than the other two types of roasts. These beans have a much lower caffeine content than light roasts do.

Dark roasts include French roast, Vienna roast, and Italian roast, among others.

PURCHASING A ROASTER

Buying a coffee roaster can be a beneficial way to start roasting your beans at home. However, knowing which roaster to pick may be challenging. Here are a few tips to keep in mind when choosing a roaster for your home use:

» Consider the speed of the roaster. If you need to get the job done fast, you'll want to pick a roaster that works faster than others.

» Consider whether or not the roaster is meant for beginners. Some are harder to use than others. Choose one that doesn't have a lot of complicated features to make it easier to learn how to work with it.

» Consider how much customization you want. Some roasters allow you to be very precise with custom settings, while others only allow you to choose between light, medium, and dark roasts.

Consider the amount of beans you want to roast at a given time. You may want to work in small batches so your beans don't become stale before you can brew them, or you may be looking for a large-batch roaster that can handle a lot at once. In general, coffee beans start losing their freshness almost as soon as they're done roasting. Standard advice is to roast and use only as many beans as you will likely consume in a two-week period. This gives you the freshest coffee for maximum enjoyment.

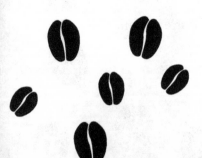

HOW TO ROAST RAW COFFEE BEANS IN A ROASTER

When you use a roaster, the process of roasting coffee beans is fairly simple. However, you'll still need to take time to practice if you want to become truly experienced enough to roast to precise temperatures and flavors. Here is the general process for roasting in a roaster:

» Follow the instruction manual that comes with your roaster to determine the right amount of beans to place inside, and then fill the roaster to the proper level.

» Turn the roaster on and roast until the beans have reached the color you're looking for. Remember that this may take some practice to get right.

» Pour the coffee out of the roaster and let it sit, stirring it a little, to cook it throughout.

» Cool and store the beans until you're ready to brew them.

ROASTING SAFETY

As with any cooking and food preparation you try at home, it's important to keep a few safety tips in mind. Remember that your coffee roaster is a heated appliance and that the beans themselves will be quite hot when you take them out of the roaster. Handle with care, and do not leave the roaster unattended while it's running. Be careful not to let the cord near water.

Roasting beans release carbon dioxide as they heat, so operate your coffee roaster in a ventilated room and don't cover any fans on the outside of the product. The CO_2 gas from coffee roasting can be dangerous, so be sure it doesn't build up in your home.

Do not open the coffee roaster while it's working. This can cause an increased risk of fire and burns as well as smoke inhalation. It should also go without saying that you should never let children use the coffee roaster.

TIPS AND TRICKS DURING AND AFTER ROASTING

Now that you know a bit about the process of coffee roasting, here are a few tips you can remember to help you make the most of the experience.

» Learn to recognize the smell of the roast you're going for.

» Stay close-by and listen for the first and second pops.

» Don't start with entirely green coffee beans when roasting at home, as they can be harder to roast and may even damage home coffee roasting machines.

» Store your coffee beans in an airtight container in a cool, dark location for best results.

ROASTING COFFEE AT HOME

Brewing coffee

in your home and putting together the perfect cup can be a fun and rewarding experience, especially if you're interested in the world of coffee. However, if you really want to try something new and a little outside the box, you might want to attempt roasting coffee yourself at home instead. If you never realized you could roast coffee in your own home, you're in luck. In this chapter, we'll give you all the information you need to get started with your home coffee roasting endeavors.

WHERE TO BUY GREEN COFFEE BEANS

Unroasted coffee beans, also referred to as green coffee beans, may be hard to find. However, knowing where to look makes it easier to find a good quality batch of green coffee. There are a few steps involved in picking good green coffee.

Choose your beans' region. Region is important to decide on before shopping, as some vendors and stores may separate products based on origin. Others may only offer beans from one location or another, as well.

Beans from Central and South America are good for beginning roasters. These beans offer mild flavors in many varieties that can be used for all sorts of roasting levels and techniques. Beans from Brazil remain a popular choice among new home roasters, particularly because these beans are sweeter than some of the other options out there. Choose a bean from this region for light and medium roasts with a few darker options.

Coffee beans from Indonesia can be a lot more affordable than those from other locations. However, this coffee has a stronger and sometimes bitter flavor, so it may not be for everyone.

You can also try roasting green coffee from other locations. However, the two mentioned here are the most common and easiest to find, so they're better for those who are just getting started.

Stick to arabica beans, especially if you're not very experienced yet. Robusta beans are a lower quality type of coffee and may not have a good flavor. It takes an experienced roaster to know how to bring out the good elements of a robusta coffee bean. However, some blends do contain a portion of these beans, and buying a blend including some robusta can help you save money. For this reason, even some new roasters don't shy away from blends.

If possible, ask the vendor about the specific flavor profile and aspects of the coffee beans you're considering. You may not always be able to find out this information, depending on where you get your beans. When you can, find out about the acidity, body, and taste of the beans.

Decide whether or not you want to buy fair trade, organic, bird-friendly, or other categories of beans. If you can afford to do so, it's a good idea to look for at least one of these options on the label.

You can order beans online, but you probably shouldn't the first time you buy green coffee. It's better to be able to smell and look at the beans before you buy them. If you do order online, be sure to stick to trusted vendors with good reviews and a positive reputation among coffee roasters.

Don't over-purchase, especially for your first time buying. Buy just enough beans to allow you to practice your roasting technique, but not so many that they'll go bad before you can get through them all. This is also a good choice in the event you end up with a bean whose taste you don't really like.

Store your beans in a cool, dry location. Keep them in an airtight container and away from heat and direct sunlight. Make sure to keep them in a place where insects and pests won't be an issue as well.

ITEMS YOU'LL NEED

Gather the needed items before you begin the roasting process. Although some of these are optional, you will need to have most of them on hand to ensure the job is as easy and smooth as possible. There's more than one method of roasting coffee beans at home, so be sure you get the items you need for the right process.

FOR OVEN ROASTING:

» Oven

» Baking pan with perforations. Make sure you don't choose a pan with large enough holes that the coffee beans can fall through them.

» Kitchen timer

» Wooden spoon or spatula

» Durable oven mitt for safety

» Metal strainer

FOR POPCORN POPPER ROASTING:

» Popcorn popper (air style popper with vents on the sides—not on the bottom)

» Bowl for catching bean skins

» Wooden spoon

» Metal strainer

OVEN ROASTING

Follow these steps to learn how to oven roast your coffee beans. This method is not as simple as the popcorn popping one listed below, but it can give you a little bit more control over the way the beans roast, as well as the flavors and aromas you can get from the beans you've chosen.

Depending on whether or not you have an electric or gas oven, the temperature you need to set for preheating may differ. It's recommended to start with 500 degrees Fahrenheit for electric and slightly lower, around 475 or so, for gas. However, you may need to adjust this to get the right roast.

Spread the beans over your baking pan so that they're all touching each other but not sitting on top of each other. Make sure they cover the "floor space" of the pan.

Open some windows and turn on some fans. You should also turn on the ventilation on your oven, but keep in mind this probably won't be enough on its own to take care of the smoke the roasting process will produce. Understand that there's a chance your smoke detectors will go off while you're roasting.

Make sure you can easily get the beans out of the oven and outdoors somewhere to cool when they're finished roasting. You need to lower their temperature quickly when they are finished roasting, so taking them outside is a good option.

After the oven finishes preheating, put the tray of beans in and shut the door. Turn on the kitchen timer and stay close to the oven.

The first few times you roast, check on the beans very frequently at first. If you notice them roasting in one spot more than in others, stir them quickly as needed. Do not open the oven door often and do not leave it open for more than a few seconds at a time.

Listen for the first pop of the beans. This will let you know that the green coffee has reached the point just before the light roast stage. If you don't want a dark roast, you'll need to take them out before you hear a second pop. However, if you want a very dark coffee, you'll need to wait for two pops.

As soon as the beans are the color you want, take them out of the oven and hurry—carefully!—to get them outside for cooling. Place them in a metal strainer and shake them gently to help cool them off and remove the skins from the outside of the beans at the same time.

It usually takes anywhere from ten to fifteen minutes to roast coffee, depending on your oven, your pan, and the roast you're looking for. It may take a lot of trial and error to get this right when using an oven, but with enough practice, you'll be roasting the perfect coffee beans right in your own kitchen in no time.

POPCORN POPPER

It's easier to roast coffee at home in a popcorn popper, although it still takes some getting used to. With a little practice, you can easily learn how to achieve the perfect roast for your coffee using this simple method.

Put your popcorn popper in a place where the smoke won't cause any major issues. Some people like doing this outside or near a window, but your oven's hood fan can sometimes be enough to deal with the smoke, too. Just like with the oven method, expect a lot of smoke and the possibility of your smoke detectors going off.

Check out the manufacturer's recommendations for how much popcorn to put in the popcorn popper at one time. Measure the same weight in coffee beans and place them in the popper.

Set the lid, butter dish, and other pieces of the popcorn popper into place as you would for normal operations. Keep in mind that it is crucial for coffee beans to stay in the popcorn popper longer than it is for popcorn kernels. You may run the risk of melting your butter dish using this method. All popcorn poppers are unique, so use your best judgment when picking one for this task.

Put a bowl or other receptacle under the popcorn chute. This is for catching the skins of the coffee beans as they get thrown off during the process.

Turn the machine on. Stay close-by so you can listen for the first popping sound, the same as you would with the oven roasting method. The same rules apply here too—one crack means you're nearing light roast, while two cracks means you're in dark roast territory. It should take only two or three minutes to hear the first pop.

About a minute after the first pop, check the beans for color and roast. Continue checking frequently until they reach the desired color.

It should take about four minutes for a light or blonde roast and up to seven minutes for a very dark espresso-style roast, with medium and medium-dark falling in between these two times. Do not leave the beans unattended, as the roast color can change very quickly.

Be sure to remove the beans from the machine just before they reach the darkness you're looking for. This will account for further cooking from the inside as they cool down to room temperature and can prevent the beans from burning, especially if you're going for a darker roast.

Place the beans in the metal strainer and stir them with a wooden spoon until they cool down to be warm enough to touch.

Be sure to remove the beans from the machine just before they reach the darkness you're looking for.

COOLING AND WAITING

No matter which means of roasting you choose, you'll need to wait for the beans to cool down before you can finish processing them. This step may be tempting to skip, but it's crucial to making sure your beans taste great and stay fresh.

The biggest reason why you need to cool your beans down quickly is because they will continue to roast from the inside out if you don't. This will quickly cause them to burn and develop bitter, sour tastes that you simply don't want in your coffee. However, they also cannot be exposed to much water at this stage, so there's no way to soak them to cool them off either.

It's widely recommended to use the metal strainer method listed in both guides above for cooling your coffee beans. Stirring the beans and allowing air to flow all around them is a good way to quickly lower their temperature. Doing this outside can help even more.

If it's very hot outside when you roast your beans, you might want to spray them very gently with cold water from a spray bottle. Do not overdo this, and always err on the side of less water if you decide to try it. When you spray the hot beans, you should see the mist from the spray bottle evaporate right away. This will work to keep them cooler without saturating them with water and ruining them.

If all else fails, roast in the morning or at night so you don't have to worry as much about heat. And keep in mind, too, that the humidity outdoors can make it harder to cool down your coffee beans in a timely manner. Don't forget to account for the weather when trying to roast at home.

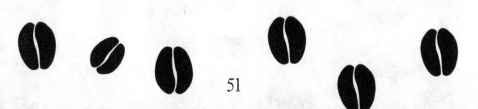

51

How to Buy and Store Coffee

Now that you've learned a little bit about what coffee is and where

it comes from, it's time to branch out into the realm of purchasing coffee for yourself. When you go to the store to buy coffee, you may think it's as simple as picking between caffeinated or decaf. However, there are some additional elements involved in the selection of coffee, and choosing a good one that will suit your needs and preferences can be tricky. In this chapter, we'll help you better understand how to buy your coffee as well as how to store it when you bring it home.

WHOLE BEAN VS. GROUND

There are two main types of coffee available for purchase: whole bean and ground. Wherever you choose to purchase your coffee beans, you'll find both options available on the shelves. Some people prefer to stick to coffee that has already been pre-ground before packaging, while others like grinding it themselves at home. There are pros and cons to both of these options, however, and it's a good idea to understand the pros and cons of each so you can make the right choice.

Take a look at the two styles of coffee and consider which one may benefit you the most.

WHOLE COFFEE BEANS

If you buy a bag of whole coffee beans, you're getting a product that's as close to fresh as possible. These beans are still in the state they were in when they left their farm, and they haven't lost much of their flavor yet. They'll still look, smell, and taste as intensely as they did right after they were finished being processed. This is the reason why many consumers prefer to buy their beans whole, so they can enjoy the coffee's flavor as it was intended—straight out of nature and into a cup.

Whole beans are a little more of a hassle than the pre-ground variety, however. When you buy whole beans, you need to think about how to store them to preserve their freshness. The point of having coffee made from whole beans is to enjoy the freshest possible taste every time you brew, so it's crucial to make the right storage decisions to ensure this can happen.

It's also a little more inconvenient to buy whole because you'll need to grind the coffee yourself. This will require a coffee grinder or some other piece of equipment as well as time to take care of the task on a regular basis.

GROUND COFFEE BEANS

As you learned in previous chapters, coffee goes through a lengthy process before it reaches the bean form most consumers recognize. As soon as the beans complete this journey—and once they are roasted—they begin to lose their flavor. In other words, coffee is perishable. The longer it sits on a farm or in a warehouse, the greater the opportunity it has to lose its freshness. Most of the time, coffee reaches buyers before it loses too much of its flavor profile. However, this is not always the case, and ground coffee may suffer the most from the natural aging process.

When coffee beans are ground, their taste and aroma both begin to escape immediately. Coffee that has been pre-ground before packaging is never going to taste or smell quite as nice as whole, fresh coffee beans. For this reason, too, ground coffee may go stale much sooner in your home than whole coffee beans might.

However, ground coffee is much more convenient to purchase, since you don't have to worry about grinding it yourself. If you don't own a coffee grinder or don't have the time to worry about grinding beans regularly, this may be a better option for you.

In the end, the choice is up to you. Some people swear by ground coffee while others only buy whole. There isn't much of a price difference between the two, so there's no budgetary reasons why you may want to pick one or the other. The biggest difference is in the taste, with shelf life and aroma also playing a part. Just remember that you'll need to purchase something for grinding your coffee if you decide to go with whole beans, and you'll need to brush up on your grinding ability as well. (More about coffee grinding later.)

For the best coffee experience, stick to whole beans.

ROASTING DATE

Coffee does not last as long as you might think it does. Many people buy big tubs of pre-ground coffee and keep it in their refrigerator, freezer, or pantry for months, slowly working through it before repeating the process again. Although this method will certainly provide you with a cup of coffee to drink every morning, it's not the best way to go about enjoying your brew. Buying coffee in bulk is not a good option unless you're planning to drink it all very quickly, as it will go bad sooner than you realize. When you want to savor your morning brew, there are better methods.

Paying attention to the roasting date on your bag of coffee can help you better keep track of how long it can be used. This date will let you know when the beans finished processing, so you can understand how long they've been sitting on the shelf before making their way to you. You have several months to enjoy the coffee before its flavor will diminish and it will start to taste stale. However, the sooner the better in most cases. As with any type of food, the beans will taste better while they're still fresh and closer to their natural form.

Remember that your coffee will change more after you open its packaging, and it will begin to experience off-gassing at this time. Some types of beans taste better after off-gassing for a few days than they do right out of the brand new bag. Espresso, for example, is better after sitting for about a week-and-a-half in a cool, dry location before you brew it. Beans intended for pour overs (pouring water directly over coffee through a filter into your cup) can benefit from sitting for a few days before you use them as well.

Bags of coffee usually also have an expiration date printed on the packaging. Although you will not get food poisoning from coffee that is past its expiration date, it will not taste its richest anymore. Technically, whole bean coffee can be kept in the freezer for nearly a year after this date, and ground coffee can stay in the freezer for many years with no cause for concern. Although old frozen coffee may do in a pinch, it's not going to give you a great taste experience, so standard coffee wisdom is to buy smaller amounts of coffee and use it up within approximately two weeks for best flavor.

ROASTER INFORMATION

The next step in choosing a good coffee is to take a look at the roaster information printed on the packaging. Sometimes, the brand name and the roaster are not the same thing—particularly if you buy your coffee locally or from a small mom-and-pop store. Even some bigger and more well-known brand names of coffee come from a roaster with a different name, though, so be sure to take your time and look closely for this information. Knowing the roaster responsible for your beans can help you figure out whether or not they're the right beans for you.

Some roasters may be just starting out. If you're thinking of buying coffee from a new roaster, there's no reason not to give it a try. Just remember that it may be lacking in the complexities of a coffee profile created by a roaster who's been at it for several years or more. On the other hand, some roasters may be relatively unknown but capable of providing very high-quality coffee with amazing tastes and smells throughout the experience. Sometimes it pays to branch out and try coffee beans from someone new. There's always some risk with doing this, but it can be well worth a try.

A very good roaster is going to be well-known, at least in the world of coffee aficionados. When you find the name of the roaster responsible for the beans you're considering, look it up online. A quick search will let you know if it's become popular or recognized for its skill and ability with beans. You may also be able to use this information to find out whether or not the roaster has been recognized formally with certifications or awards for product, practices, or both. Some may even be celebrated outside the coffee industry, too.

In some cases, the beans you're thinking about buying may not tell you the name of the roaster. If this happens, there may be one of two reasons. The first possibility is that the name on the bag is the same as the roaster's name. The second, however, is that the roaster may not be well-known enough to get a place on the bag. This is usually common in lower budget coffee, but again, the experience can vary depending on the brand and bag. If the identity of the roaster matters to you, it may be better to skip those coffees that do not provide you this information.

ORIGIN

There are many possible origins of coffee. Beans that come from different locations taste differently due to environmental factors, and some consumers prefer one location's flavors over the others. Choosing the right coffee for your needs may be a little easier when you determine which origins you like the most. A quality bag of beans will tell you somewhere on the packaging where it comes from. If you buy your coffee from a café or a specialty shop, the employees or baristas should be able to give you this information as well.

Some of the most common origins you may find in your coffee enjoyment experiences include the following:

BRAZIL. These coffees have bold flavors and lots of elements in every sip.

HAWAII. This type of bean is lighter and smells more fragrant than other types.

ETHIOPIA. All sorts of coffees come from this region, from light to dark and from mild to bold. They span many tastes and styles.

COLOMBIA. These are milder, lighter roasts than some of the others found worldwide.

KENYA. This type of coffee isn't for everyone, as it can be sour and bitter. However, many people enjoy this unique twist on the classic brew and go out of their way to buy Kenyan coffee beans.

Remember that you may also want to consider environmental friendliness, green practices, bird safety, and fair trade when choosing your coffee. These factors can help you narrow down your selection and pick a product you can feel good about buying with an origin that isn't harmful to the world around you. More and more consumers are reaching for coffees that meet one or more of these requirements, so you may want to take this opportunity to give them a try for yourself, too.

STORAGE OPTIONS

If you've always been the type of person to throw your coffee beans in the freezer without a second thought, here are some tips to help you make better storage decisions.

Buy less coffee at a time to ensure it stays fresh as long as you need it to.

It's okay to keep coffee in an open, room temperature container for a few days. However, after about a week, it will start to degrade in quality, so only do this if you know you'll be using it soon enough.

Keep coffee beans and pre-ground coffee both in airtight, sealed containers. Store them away from sunlight and in a cool, dry location.

When you need to grind beans, only grind enough for the coffee you'll be drinking that day. This way, you can use them while they're still fresh and the taste is optimal.

If you do choose to freeze your coffee, make sure the container you use is completely airtight to prevent freezer burn. This will also keep the coffee from picking up any unpleasant flavors and smells from the freezer and the other food around it.

Plastic and glass containers can both work for coffee, but plastic may cause strange odors after a while.

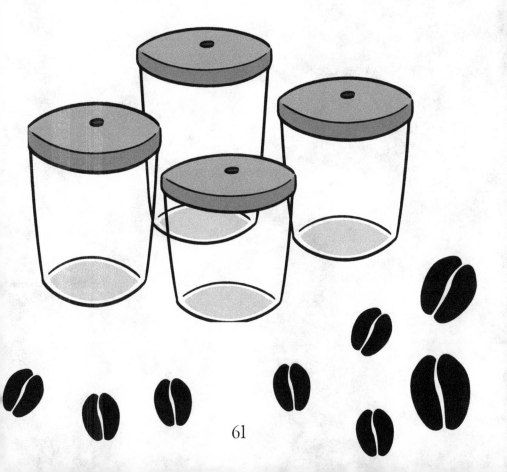

HOW TO TASTE COFFEE

Did you know

you can practice coffee tasting the same way you'd try wine tasting? Enjoying a cup of coffee can mean so much more than just guzzling it down and moving on to the next activity for the day, but it takes a little practice and know-how to get it right. When you understand the process for coffee tasting, you can learn more about your own preferences and the flavors that stand out to you with every cup. This can also be a nice way to bond with fellow coffee fans and to share your knowledge with others, too.

In this chapter, we'll walk you through the steps you need to take to enjoy a coffee tasting experience unlike any you've ever had before. You can try this with any coffee you have on hand, but you're more likely to find complexities and subtle notes among specialty coffees and those that come from whole beans. With time, you can learn to identify or at least narrow down origins of your coffee based on the way they taste, and you will come to understand more about how to buy and enjoy the beans you love by exploring various coffee tastes.

BREATHE IT IN

You probably already know that taste begins with your nose. When you smell something, it helps you get a better idea of what to expect from the flavor, and it can even help increase the tastes that go along with the food or drink in question. Coffee is no different, and smelling it before you drink it can make a big difference in the way you enjoy your sips. You can start smelling coffee as soon as you open the container of beans, and this is widely recommended as the starting point for the true enjoyment of any brew.

After you smell the beans, grind them according to your preferences and needs. Next, smell the ground coffee once again, and take the time to notice how the aroma has changed as the form of the coffee was altered. The same main notes should still be there, but there will be some elements that mellowed out after grinding and others that came to the front of the profile. This is also a good time to write down anything you might want to remember about what you're enjoying as you smell the first few steps of the coffee, too.

If you're making your coffee as a pour over, wet the grounds a little as per the pour over method. Before you continue, lean in and smell the wet grounds just a little bit. You don't have to take long for this step, as taking too much time will negatively impact the pour over experience. However, you should at least notice the way the grounds change once again when they are exposed to water.

Finally, when the cup of coffee is ready for you to drink it, tilt the cup so that you get a full whiff of the smell and really breathe it in. This last, most important part of the first stage, can get your mouth and tongue ready for the experience of drinking the coffee.

SIP SLOWLY

Most coffee fans and pros look for a handful of flavor types and elements in each sip of coffee. As you begin sipping, take your time and process the taste throughout your whole mouth. Swish the coffee around like you would with wine so you can experience the way it hits each part of your tongue differently. Just as with wine, many specialty coffees are made to evoke different responses depending on how you enjoy them. Here are some of the elements to be on the lookout for:

CLEAN FLAVOR. This means that, when you swallow the coffee, the bitter aftertaste isn't going to hang around in your mouth. Most coffees do leave a little bit of a flavor on the tongue and in the mouth as a whole, but a solidly good cup of coffee shouldn't do this. It should not make your breath stale with coffee taste, and it shouldn't leave you with a sour or smoky feeling in your mouth either. It should leave your mouth feeling clean and ready to move on to another sip or to a bite of your food instead.

ACIDITY. This term refers to any coffees that provide a flavor including lemon, tomato, or blueberry. Although you may not realize it, there are actually a lot of coffee variations that make use of these types of flavors. Some coffees have acidity due to the ingredients used in brewing or processing, while others may get theirs from the weather and climate in the location where the beans are grown. The term acidity, in this case, does not refer to the pH level of the coffee and only describes flavor.

SWEETNESS. Many coffee beans have a sweetness to them, and most of the time, you can even smell it at least a little bit in the whole bean. When you sip the coffee, are you able to locate different sweet sources throughout the flavor profile? Can you find the taste of mocha or chocolate, which is very common in some dark roasts especially? Or are you picking up on honey, caramel, or maple? Just as with acidity, the location and means of production of the beans can affect the sweetness of the coffee, as can the roast and even the grind.

BODY. Another term for this is "mouthfeel," although it's not often used to describe coffee as much as alcohols and liquors. Is the coffee very watery, or does it have a fullness to it when you take a sip? Does it sit in the mouth a certain way, or does it go down smoothly? Can you identify that the coffee is a dark, medium, or light roast simply based on the body, and can you consider the body of the drink when determining how it was ground and brewed too?

TAKE A DRINK

Now that you've taken your time in identifying smells, tastes and textures going on in your cup, it's time to actually sit back and take a drink. You shouldn't sip your way through the entire mug of coffee, but you should give yourself plenty of time to really work through the contemplation of the drink before moving on to the full drinking stage. This way, you'll learn to identify the flavors you like and pick out the ones that aren't working for you very well. In doing this, you'll have a better relationship with coffee and how you drink it, and you'll know what to expect from your favorite beans, too.

When you take a drink of your coffee, there's no need to chug it. In fact, if the coffee is very rich and bold, you may want to avoid chugging it altogether, as it could disrupt your tasting experience. Take a normal drink of the brew and see how the various tones you picked out in the previous step work together. How do they dance with each other, and where do some of the flavors stand out more than the others? Are you still noticing the same tastes you picked up on before, and is the original aroma of the whole bean still making its presence known?

When you get to the bottom of the mug, are some of the grounds still floating there? If so, you may not have chosen the right brewing method or picked the right grind. The coffee should be smooth and consistent throughout the whole experience, and if the last sip is unpleasant compared to the rest, something may need to be tweaked somewhere along the way. This is part of the trial and error of coffee brewing, so don't be discouraged if something went a little wrong.

CONSIDER THE FLAVOR PALATE

Thinking about the flavor palate of your coffee involves asking yourself several questions. These questions can help you determine the different elements involved in both the beans and the brew, and they can also make it easier for you to pick out things you like and dislike in the world of coffee tasting. This way, the next time you go shopping for a new style of beans, you'll know more than just, "I like blonde roasts," or, "I'm not into medium roasts." Here are a few questions to ask yourself at the end of your cup of coffee to finish off the tasting experience:

> » Did I notice more than a couple of flavors going on together? If so, did the flavors work well with each other, or did some of them stick out in a bad way?

> » Did I notice layers of flavoring, or did everything land the same way on my tongue? Were there stages of each sip, or did it feel too repetitive working through the cup?

> » As the coffee got cooler, did the flavor change? If it changed, was it for better or worse? Did it get bitter and taste old after it got colder, or did the flavors become something new and equally enjoyable?

GRINDING COFFEE
SUCCESSFULLY

As with most aspects of enjoying coffee, you

can handle this one the easy way or the hard way. Sticking to ease
and convenience is fine if all you're looking for in your cup of coffee
is something to wake you up on your way to work every morning.
However, if you truly want to be able to sit back, relax, and relish
in that brew, it's going to take more than a quick chop in a coffee
grinder to get your beans ready for tasting. By understanding the ins
and outs of grinding your coffee beans at home, you can set yourself
up for a better result every time you pour yourself a mug.

In this chapter, you'll learn how to pick the right type of grinder for
your coffee, as well as what to do if you don't have a grinder at all.
You'll also find out which grind level is right for different styles of
coffee brewing, even if you're interested in trying less common or
more elaborate techniques and methods. This may seem like a lot of
complicated information, but with a little practice and learning, you
can easily start making coffee that is ground to perfection before
you even add water.

CHOOSE THE RIGHT GRINDER

The first step in getting your coffee to the perfect grind every time is to make sure you're working with the proper grinding method. There aren't a lot of different types of coffee grinders out there, but the varieties that are available to you can make a difference in the flavor of the coffee you brew. When you go to the store to buy a grinder, you may be a little overwhelmed by the different selections available. Take a look at our tips below to help you keep track of which kind is which.

STANDARD BURR GRINDER

This is one of the most common types of coffee grinder on the market. It comes in at about mid-range in terms of pricing. The standard type of Burr grinder is the plate grinder, and this variant utilizes two flat disks that spin continually and press together to mash the coffee beans into the right consistency for brewing. These are very precise appliances that can allow you to pick from a wide variety of different levels and settings. However, their biggest flaw is that they get a little too warm and have been known to burn the coffee beans or cause them to taste a little smoky.

BLADED GRINDER

When you think of a coffee grinder, chances are good this is the type you imagine. This is the cheapest style on the market and it is a very basic solution to whole bean grinding needs. All you have to do is fill it with beans, close the lid, plug it in, and let it do its job. It works by rotating sharp blades inside the main housing chamber and cutting up your coffee beans as it does so. You can control the degree of your grind from coarse to fine by the length of time you run the blades. After a bit of practice you'll know how long to operate your grinder to get the grind you like. This type of grinder is a little harder to keep clean, but not overly so—a stiff bristled brush and a damp cloth will do the trick.

CONICAL BURR GRINDER

This is a different style of the standard Burr grinder listed above. It is the most expensive type of home coffee grinder and is generally the best as well. This is an electric product that allows you to set the grind to the level and style you want, push a button, and let the appliance do the work for you. It's easy to keep this type of grinder clean by taking it apart and rinsing or scrubbing the individual pieces as needed, and it's also easy to learn how to use this item, too. It's a great choice for beginners who aren't sure about how to precisely control other options from this list, and it's good for old pros who want to branch out in their coffee experiences too.

HAND CRANK GRINDER

Another affordable mid-range solution is a hand crank grinder. This an old-fashioned product that has started to come back into fashion among some coffee fans. To operate one of these items, you must place beans inside and manually turn the crank. This takes a long time and is rather difficult, so it is not ideal for those who are in a hurry or anyone that doesn't want a workout along with their morning cup. However, when looking for a way to show off to friends and family, or you want to buy a unique present for a coffee lover in your life, this can be a good alternative to other grinders.

CHOOSE THE RIGHT GRIND LEVEL

The next stage of this experience is to choose the right grinding level for the coffee you're making. In other words, you're picking the grind that's right for the type of coffee maker you have. If you don't have a coffee maker and you're planning to brew your coffee using another method, then it's even more crucial to choose the type of grind that's meant for the style of beverage you want to create. This can take some getting used to, but with practice, you'll be able to determine the right method of grinding for just about any type of coffee.

THERE ARE THREE KINDS OF GRINDS.

COARSE: This grind looks like coffee beans that haven't been chopped up very much, and that's pretty accurate. Its appearance is similar to dirt, and individual pieces are all big enough to see. Within broader "coarse" terminology, grounds may be either standard or extra-coarse. Extra-coarse will look even more distinct and have larger chunks than the standard.

MEDIUM: Next up is medium. This looks more uniform in terms of the sizes of the individual pieces, but you can still tell them apart from each other by looking. When you pour it, this coffee looks like sand moving through an hourglass. The pieces should all be more or less the same size. One good way to match a medium grind is to compare it to store-bought coffee grounds. Unless otherwise specified, this type of coffee is almost always ground to medium.

FINE: Fine grinds look and feel similar to sugar. They are hard to tell apart from each other when you look at the finished product, and they may be so fine that they would pass through certain types of coffee filters and products. If you've ever bought pre-ground espresso, chances are good you've come across finely ground coffee at least once. Most espresso beans that are sold already ground to fit into the finely ground category, although some may lean a little more toward medium fine.

There are also another two styles to keep in mind.

SUPER FINE: This grind is extremely fine, but when you rub it between your fingers you can still feel the texture of sugar granules. This is only meant for certain types of coffees and shouldn't be used for the more common variations you're likely to be brewing.

TURKISH GRIND: This method is specifically meant for making Turkish coffee. In this grind, the beans are broken down into a powder with a consistency similar to flour. It is much different than other grinds and isn't really intended for any other type of coffee because of this.

Each method of brewing coffee can be divided into a different grind category.

COARSE: Use coarsely ground coffee for French press and vacuum style coffee makers. This is also the best choice for a percolator.

MEDIUM: Auto drip coffee makers—like the ones you can find in most household kitchens—use medium grinds. You may want to go with a medium to fine grind if your coffee maker has a cone filter instead of a flat one.

FINE: Espresso pots and espresso machines utilize fine coffee grinds. You may also choose a fine grind if you have a conical drip filter, instead of a medium-fine grind. These coffee makers can usually work with both interchangeably.

SUPER FINE: This style is best for espresso machines that require very small granules of coffee in order to function properly.

TURKISH: You should only use this grind for making Turkish coffee, as it's too fine and powdery to work otherwise.

GRINDING COFFEE WITHOUT A GRINDER

What happens when you want to drink freshly-ground coffee but don't want to buy a grinder? Is it even possible to make coffee from whole beans without something to grind it as part of your kitchen appliance ensemble? When you have access to whole beans but not a coffee grinder, you do have options. Take a look at the list below to help you figure out the best way to grind and enjoy your coffee beans even if you don't own a grinder and don't want to purchase one.

HAMMER

If you've never thought of beating up your coffee beans with a hammer, now's your chance to give it a try. This is a somewhat dangerous method, so be careful not to try it on a fragile countertop or table, and take care to keep your fingers safely out of the way. Put the beans on a piece of parchment paper over a sturdy surface. Use the hammer (or a meat tenderizer) to break down the beans to the right consistency. You should get a coarse grind out of this.

MORTAR AND PESTLE

If you're into making your own ground spices at home, you may already have a mortar and pestle. If you don't have one, they're usually more affordable than coffee grinders. Place a small amount of beans in the mortar and crush them with the pestle, twisting as you go to make sure the beans break up as they should. Continue rolling and moving the coffee around in the mortar until it is the right grind for your needs.

ROLLING PIN

Spread some parchment paper over a big cutting board and fold the edges to make a pocket for keeping the coffee in one location. Spread a small amount of the beans out over the paper and use the rolling pin to crush them. Press down firmly while pushing the rolling pin back and forth across the beans.

BLENDER

You can get a grind similar to what you'd find with a blade style grinder by using your blender. Remember, however, that not all blenders have blades that are strong enough to handle coffee beans. Some have a coffee-specific setting, and others are capable of processing coffee but don't specify this. Be sure to read the blender's instruction manual to find out more. It's best to pulse your blender rather than to turn it on a specific setting so you can better keep track of the grind. You should be able to achieve a standard coarse-to-medium finish when you use a blender.

KNIFE

Finally, you can use a knife in a manner similar to the hammer and rolling pin methods if you want to. Put the beans on a sturdy cutting board and spread them out evenly. You should not try to chop the beans, but instead lay the knife on its side and use the flat portion to crush the beans to the grind you're looking for. You can get almost any level of grind from this method, including coarse, medium, and fine. With practice, you may even be able to crush espresso beans to the right texture by utilizing a knife.

METHODS OF BREWING

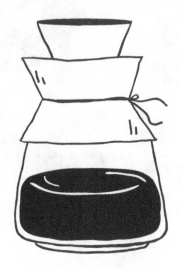

Most people

know there are several ways to brew a good cup of coffee, but how do you know which one is really right for you? Some people prefer one method over others, and some are happy to change between different methods depending on their mood, day, or time of the year. Familiarize yourself with the most common (and some more uncommon) methods of brewing to easily pick the one you'll enjoy the most. Try choosing different brews as you learn and grow.

DRIP FILTERS

A classic drip filter is ideal for most types of coffee. These are the types of coffee makers you can find in most kitchens (and diners), and they have become so popular for good reason. They brew coffee quickly and can make a very good cup in most instances. They're easy to clean, small enough to fit on most kitchen counters, and aren't nearly as expensive as some of the other choices out there. They come in many varieties, colors, and styles to suit most needs, making them a good all-around choice.

You probably already have experience operating a classic electric coffee maker. Basically, the appliance receives water to a certain volume depending on how much coffee is needed. A paper filter is put in place for holding ground coffee. Water is pumped into the filter, which drips through the ground coffee, and is caught in a carafe below. This product makes a bubbling sound synonymous for many people with waking up in the morning.

These coffee makers can be a great choice for medium grinds. They may seem a little too ordinary, but you can make a very good cup of coffee using this type of product. They are not designed to handle coarse grinds (which can clog up the filter and the machine), nor can they deal with fine grinds (that can simply be pushed through the filter and contaminate the coffee). But for medium grinds, there's no reason to break the bank on complicated machinery. As an added bonus, high-quality water yields even better results.

FRENCH PRESS

The French press is an older coffee making method that has recently seen a comeback in popularity. Coffee is relatively consistent when made in a press. Pressing extracts oils and caffeine content from beans in a more uniform way than other methods, and helps the coffee taste better and wake you up more quickly at the same time. This method isn't for everyone, but it's a good choice for those looking to get a little something different out of their regular cup.

You must use coarse ground beans in a French press to ensure the press works as it should and doesn't become damaged. Place grounds in a press pot along with the correct volume of water. You may need to let it sit for one or two minutes, or you may be able to start pressing right away—be sure to read the manufacturer's instructions to find out for sure. Press the coffee plunger down slowly to force the brewed coffee through the built-in filter and allow it to drip into a receptacle. This takes about four minutes.

If you're looking for a more portable and convenient French press option, you can choose the AeroPress. This product does use a filter and relies on a lot of elbow grease to push the plunger down. It can work in a pinch, but it is a little pricey and may not be ideal for regular daily use. It may also not make as consistent a cup of coffee as the regular press pot can.

POUR OVER

A pour over works in more or less the same way as a classic drip coffee filter, but it is a manual process instead of an electric one. This method is very low cost and is a great solution for anyone who wants to enjoy the full flavor and aroma of a cup of coffee without spending a fortune to make that happen. It's also ideal for people living in smaller spaces who don't have room to devote to larger coffee makers or espresso machines. You can find pour over items for as little as about ten dollars, or you can get nicer ones made of better materials for much higher prices, depending on what you're looking for.

To make a pour over cup of coffee, you must first set up the coffee cone over a receptacle. The cone and receptacle are usually sold together, but not always. The shape and style of the cone, as well as the material it's made of, can make a difference in the way the coffee will taste when it's finished brewing. When the cone is set up and in place, you must then put a filter in place as well. You have to buy the right type of paper filter for the cone you've chosen. Place about three tablespoons of ground coffee in the paper filter inside the cone and make sure it's tapped down into the cone, but not pressed firmly together. Heat water to just before boiling, then pour it gently and slowly over the coffee in the filter. It's best to start pouring a little, stop and wait for the coffee to bubble, and then continue pouring. The coffee will drip through the filter and be ready to drink in about three minutes.

There are many different styles of pour over products you can choose from. Depending on the material and shape you like, you may be able to find some easily, while others can be pricey and tough to come by. Chemex is a very popular choice among pour overs, but it is a little more expensive than most others and relies on a specific type of filter in order to work properly. However, if you want to try the upper end of quality for your next pour over, Chemex is the way to go.

TURKISH COFFEE

Turkish coffee is becoming more and more popular in recent years, and if you've never tried it, then you may want to take time to check it out. This type of coffee is surrounded by ritual and culture, so it can be beneficial to your appreciation of the drink to read up on the background of the brew and learn what it means to those who have been drinking it for centuries. You will need some specific materials and items to make this type of coffee, and it may take a little longer to brew than some other methods.

To begin with, you need very finely ground coffee. You should choose coffee that has been ground so much that it is like powder or flour. Any other type is not going to work. You can grind it yourself or look for pre-ground coffee that is labeled for Turkish coffee purposes.

Add a cup of cold water and a pinch of sugar to a very small saucepan and bring to a boil over medium heat. Take the boiled water off the heat as soon as it boils and add a tablespoon of the ground coffee and a pinch or two of ground cardamom. Stir very gently and then return to the heat. Let it boil once again, and take the coffee off the heat when it starts to foam and bubble on top. Let it settle for a few seconds, then repeat the process, removing the coffee again from the heat when it starts to foam. Pour the coffee out into a small cup and let it stand for a couple of minutes before drinking. This will allow the grounds to sink to the bottom and will make the flavors much more pleasant as well. Do not stir your coffee after you pour it.

ESPRESSO MACHINE

Espresso machines are only intended for use with espresso beans that have been ground to the right consistency for espresso shots. They cannot be used to brew a regular cup of coffee, and trying to do this can damage your machine as well as ruin your drink. If you want to pull espresso shots, then you will need an espresso machine. However, if you don't, then it's better to skip this expensive and complicated piece of equipment.

If you are looking to buy an espresso machine, remember that you can find several models and styles to suit your needs. A true espresso machine is a large piece of equipment that is very expensive and comes with all the bells and whistles you need to make the perfect shot every time. However, it is possible to find much smaller machines that can pull a shot or two of espresso at once and maybe steam milk as well. These machines are usually plenty for home espresso enthusiasts to enjoy.

PERCOLATOR AND COWBOY COFFEE

Coffee hobbyists tend to neglect the percolator as a viable way to brew coffee at home. However, depending on the flavor and style you're looking for in your drink, this may be exactly what you need. Percolators were popular many decades ago, but they're still available if you know where to shop for them, and they can be an interesting and fun addition to a coffee fan's kitchen. Buying a quality percolator is important, as some are made a little bit worse than others and may not provide you with the taste you want. Choose a metal percolator for best results.

To percolate coffee, you first must fill the bottom of the product with enough water to make the volume of coffee you need. Try to get this measurement as exact as possible to prevent your coffee from being too strong or too watered down. Attach the filter to the percolator and put in the right amount of coffee grounds—one tablespoon for about every eight ounces of water. Put the top portion of the percolator on and close the lid. Put the percolator on your stove over medium heat until it is very hot but is not boiling yet. You may need to adjust the heat as you go to keep the water from boiling or the coffee from brewing too fast.

Once the water reaches a point where it's making a few bubbles every now and then, it's ready. Turn off the heat but leave the percolator on the hot burner for about ten minutes (or less if you prefer a milder coffee). Take the percolator apart so you can access the coffee inside. Although this process is a little more involved than some others, it is environmentally friendly and is ideal for camping too.

Cowboy coffee works much like coffee made in a percolator. Make this coffee by putting water in a stovetop pot. The amount of water you choose will depend on how much coffee you want in the end. Boil over medium heat, then remove as soon as it boils. Leave it alone for 30 seconds. Measure out two tablespoons of coffee for every cup and add directly to the pot. Use only finely ground coffee for this purpose. Stir, then let stand for two minutes, and then stir once more. Leave it alone for another two minutes and then drizzle a small amount of cold water over the top. Pour carefully so grounds do not get into the drink.

Cowboy coffee isn't the best or most delicious way to make coffee, but some people enjoy trying it every now and then, especially for a fun twist on the more common methods. It's also a good choice for camping, since you only need a fire and a pot to make a good, strong cup of coffee just about anywhere.

CHOOSING THE RIGHT WATER FOR BREWING

Picking the right water for brewing your coffee is one of the key factors in making the perfect cup. Some types of water simply aren't cut out for coffee brewing. If you're interested in making a cup of coffee the recommended way, you should understand the different water types and issues you may encounter when trying to do so. While there's nothing stopping you from making coffee with water right out of the tap, there are some compelling reasons why you might prefer to choose something of a better quality, and a little more filtered, before you start working on your morning brew.

SOFT VS. HARD WATER

Hard and soft water are both terms that can describe any water with a pH balance other than neutral. While it's always nice to have pH balanced water, most of the time it's not really possible to have it right out of your tap. Most homes have either hard or soft water, and it's important to find out which your home has before deciding whether or not to use your tap water for brewing coffee. Both of these types of water conditions pose different challenges when making coffee, but they can both be rectified as well.

Hard water is another term for water that has a higher mineral content. This water also naturally has a higher pH due to the presence of hard minerals, including magnesium and calcium. If water is only slightly hard, these minerals may actually add to the flavors in the coffee and bring out some of the subtleties a little bit more. Many people prefer to brew their coffee with slightly hard water for this reason. However, if the water is too hard, the calcium and magnesium present within it will build up on your espresso machine or coffee maker and can cause damage over time.

Soft water, on the other hand, has a lower pH and doesn't contain nearly as many minerals naturally. If you use a water softener in your home to soften your water, it may replace these minerals with sodium. Too much sodium in your softened water may make it taste a little salty, which can negatively impact the flavor of your coffee. Using sodium instead of hard water minerals may also make the water—and therefore the coffee you make with it—taste weak and unappealing.

If you must choose between the two, somewhat hard water is better than soft for coffee brewing.

FILTERED TAP WATER

Tap water is the worst choice for brewing coffee, since it's full of unwanted pollutants, contaminants, sediments, and other issues. You shouldn't put it in your coffee maker or espresso machine, as it can eventually cause clogs and damage the inner workings of the appliance. In most places, it's also not very safe to consume the tap water without filtering out at least some of the substances that are found in it.

Using a pitcher filter can help you get enough water for your coffee maker at any given time. These filters can remove chlorine and improve the taste and smell of your water. A sink faucet filter can remove a little more and may be a better option if you make a lot of coffee, or if you want filtered drinking water instead. You can also choose to install an under-sink water filter to help improve the quality of all the water that comes out of the specific sink in question.

Finally, if you really want to improve your home's water, you can put in a whole house water filter. These filter systems come in many different varieties and can remove many impurities as well as bacteria and dangerous substances from your water. They are not cheap, but they can keep you healthier while making your water taste better too. And when your water tastes better, so will your coffee—which is just a nice added bonus.

BOTTLED WATER

Bottled water is a better choice for coffee than tap water is. However, there are some issues to keep in mind when trying to choose the right bottled water for your needs, too. Some bottled waters may be more alkaline than others, and some may contain higher mineral content than others. Some are nothing more than glorified tap water, while others are very high-quality water that is well worth the price—and worth brewing into a cup of coffee every now and then. You may need to practice a little trial and error to find the right bottled water.

You should never use water that is labeled as "distilled" or "purified" for this purpose. Only pick water that says "drinking," "spring," or "artesian" on it. Water labeled as mineral water is also usually safe. And it may go without saying, but don't put sparkling or flavored water in your coffee.

REVERSE OSMOSIS WATER

Reverse osmosis is a water treatment option that takes almost all of the minerals out of the water before drinking. Some people believe this is a better way to treat the tap water in a home, but unfortunately, reverse osmosis also removes the good minerals from the water along with the unwanted ones. This is not only bad for your health, but also bad for your taste buds, as the water may be unpleasant and can lead to a badly brewed cup of coffee. Reverse osmosis water has nothing in it to bring out the natural flavors of your coffee.

Some of the more elaborate reverse osmosis filtration systems on the market will add the desirable minerals back into your water after removing contaminants and pollutants. These are very expensive and hard to come by, though, so chances are good your home is not fitted with one of these filters. If you are thinking of installing a reverse osmosis filter and want to pick something that's better for you as well as for your coffee, choose one that adds the minerals back to the water. Just remember that your coffee may be a little lacking if you use this type of water.

Only pick water that says "drinking," "spring," or "artesian" on it. Water labeled as mineral water is also usually safe.

EXPERIENCE ESPRESSO:
NOT ALL BEANS ARE THE SAME

Espresso and coffee—two of the most popular ways to wake up, start the day, or relax and enjoy some quiet time. No matter how you choose to drink your caffeinated beverage, you probably have a favorite between these two, right? They may seem like they're vastly different from each other, but really, espresso and coffee have many similarities too. In this chapter, we'll explore the ways these two types of beans differ, as well as how to choose the right kind of espresso for your favorite drinks. You'll also learn how to brew espresso at home, whether you prefer to use a machine or stick to a pour over.

HOW IS ESPRESSO DIFFERENT FROM COFFEE?

Espresso and coffee are actually more alike than they are different, even though that may be difficult to believe! Most of the differences are aesthetic ones, in that they affect the appearance, flavor, and smell of the coffee. The beans themselves, however, still come from the same plant as all other types of coffee, and they are effectively the same product. And when it comes to caffeine, the similarities are stronger—a serving of coffee and a proportional serving of espresso have around the same caffeine content. Things get a little different between the two when you consider the brewing method as well as the processing method. Here is a list of some of the ways espresso and coffee are different from one another:

Espresso is brewed much differently than coffee. There are many ways to make a brewed cup of coffee, but when it comes to espresso, the method must include speed and pressure. Water is sent through the ground espresso quickly in order to brew this beverage. This is why you must have an espresso machine if you want to make real espresso. On the other hand, if you want to make a pour over of regular coffee, you need only to gently pour hot water over the ground coffee and allow it to drip into a cup.

You can make espresso as a pour over as well. Some coffee fans will tell you that isn't "real" espresso, while others say it is just as acceptable. In reality, the decision is up to you, so find the method you enjoy the most, regardless of the argument.

Whereas coffee can be ground to several different consistencies and can come in many roasts and flavors, espresso is more specific. In order to qualify as espresso (and to be able to be brewed in an espresso machine), beans must be ground finely and have an extremely dark roast. If the grind is too coarse, the espresso will not have the full flavor and body it is meant to have. On the other hand, if it's too fine, the coffee will be much too bitter.

If you're making espresso as a pour over, you will want to go for a slightly coarser grind, somewhere in the medium range. This will prevent the coffee from seeping through the filter during the process.

Finally, espresso can be used in several types of drinks, while coffee is really only intended for a few options. Coffee can be enjoyed straight (or with milk and sugar), Americano, or iced. There aren't really any other variants on it in terms of drinks you may find on the menu at a café. Espresso, however, can be used to make drinks including cappuccino, macchiatos, flat whites, lattes, and much more. The rich, smooth flavor of espresso pairs well with milk and holds flavors nicely, so it's better suited to these types of drinks than traditional brewed coffee.

CHOOSING THE RIGHT ESPRESSO

Picking a good espresso will help you find a flavor you enjoy working with. And when you choose the right beans for your brew, it will be easier to work through the process of learning to make espresso, too. Anytime you go to a store or café selling espresso beans, you may feel a little overwhelmed by the selection. However, once you get the hang of it, picking the perfect beans will be a snap.

Keep these tips in mind when shopping for beans for your espresso:

All beans can be used for drip coffee, but not all beans can be used for espresso. You can make drip coffee using beans that have been labeled espresso. The term "espresso" on a bag of coffee simply means that the roaster, farm, or company feels that these beans are best used in espresso beverages. On the other hand, if you have a bag of non-espresso coffee beans, you cannot use them in place of espresso. They may not hold up to the brewing method, and they may be too weak to carry the flavor of the milk.

Single origin is more expensive than blends. Single origin coffee is any bean that comes from just one location. A coffee blend is made up of beans from more than one place. Blends are cheaper, because the base bean can be a lower quality or more affordable option, while the beans used to accent and add to the flavor may be higher quality. There is nothing wrong with using either of these options, and it's important to pick the one you like the best. Although single

96

origin is more popular among regular coffee, blends are still the go-to choice for espresso in most situations.

There are many shades of dark roasted coffee. Just because a coffee is dark does not make it an espresso. However, espresso must be dark. You can usually choose a dark bean that's on the lighter side for espresso if you like, but the darker options will yield bolder and more flavorful results. This choice is up to you, but remember that medium and light roasts may not work at all.

The rich, smooth flavor of espresso pairs well with milk and holds flavors nicely

Flavored or unflavored is up to you. Some espresso beans have flavors while others are strictly going to taste like the beans themselves. There's nothing wrong with choosing a flavored bean if you like it. However, remember that traditional espresso is not made with flavored beans, so it's important to choose the right type for the drink and situation. Don't forget, too, that many flavored coffee are not dark roasts.

HOW TO BREW ESPRESSO

The best and most well-known method of brewing espresso is to use an espresso machine. Some of these machines are electric and automated, while others are manual. Some hook into a water supply line while others rely on you to fill the reservoir every time you want to pull a shot. There are so many differences among espresso machines that it's important to read through the instruction manual on yours. This will help you learn the ins and outs of operating your own machine as well as keeping up with its maintenance.

Read through these directions to learn how to brew an espresso shot using the most common variant of espresso machine.

» Heat up the espresso machine about a half hour ahead of time. Take this time to pour water into the machine if needed and ensure there is a filter in place.

» Pull a shot of water to warm up the equipment and flush the nozzle.

» Remove the filter and put it on a digital food scale. Zero out the scale. Add seven grams of ground espresso to the filter.

» Using a tamp, press the espresso down into the filter to "seal" it.

» Place the filter into the head of the espresso machine, then turn on the machine.

» If your machine is not automatic, you'll need to watch carefully. Stop the espresso shot at 20 seconds for best results.

» Your espresso should be turning lightly blonde in color when you stop the shot. When finished, it should be dark on the bottom and have a crema on top. A crema is a short, frothy section you can see when you look at the espresso, similar to the head on beer.

» If you prefer your espresso as a pour over, the method is not all that different from making pour over coffee. Remember, though, that it will take longer to wait for your espresso to brew this way, and that some types of espresso beans may not be strong enough to be used in milk-based coffee drinks when made via pour over.

Follow these directions to brew up a hot cup of espresso using the less common pour over method.

» Heat water to 200 degrees Fahrenheit. Wet the filter slightly.

» Choose a grind that is intended for pour overs instead of a grind for espresso machines.

» Add the ground coffee to the filter and pour in just enough water to cover. Stir gently.

» Wait for the water to stop bubbling, then begin pouring water in the center of the grounds, spreading to the outside in a circle. Continue this for three minutes.

» Your pour over espresso should be ready to drink. Note that you won't see a crema when you brew espresso this way.

COMBINING ESPRESSO
AND MILK

Once you have learned the right way to brew your

espresso and you know how to pull a shot from your espresso machine, it's time to start branching out with drinks based on this brew. You can start by learning the basics that make up any great espresso beverage. You'll need to perfect the art of pulling the right shot for a given drink, but you'll also need to understand how to handle the milk component in these beverages. In this chapter, you'll learn how to combine milk and espresso in various ways to create some of your favorite café drinks without ever having to leave the comfort of your own home.

LATTES

The quintessential espresso-based hot drink is the latte. If you've ever gone to a café for a specialty drink, chances are good you've tried a latte before. Whether you're a latte connoisseur or this will be your first time experiencing one, you can learn how to put one together easily by following these simple instructions.

A latte contains more milk than most other types of espresso drinks. Traditionally, it is made with whole or 2% milk, but depending on your preferences and health needs, you can make it with any type, including soy or almond milk. A latte is known in some parts of the world as café au lait or grand crème.

To begin, use your espresso machine to pull a single shot of espresso. There's no need to aim for a longer or shorter shot unless you just want to; a traditional shot will work just fine. Pull the shot directly into the cup you'll be using.

If you're going to be using any flavored syrups, now is the time to add them. For a single serving latte, it's best to only use one or two pumps of syrup unless you just want an incredibly sweet drink.

You can also add sugar at this stage and allow it to dissolve in the hot espresso. Try not to over stir the espresso shot. If possible, however, do not use granulated sugar and instead go with liquid cane sugar. This will improve the flavor and consistency of the latte.

Next, pour enough milk into your espresso machine's steaming pitcher to make up the equivalent of at least two shots. You can add more if you're using a larger cup, but don't overdo it too much or the drink is going to taste like milk with a little coffee flavoring.

Steam the milk until microbubbles begin to form. You should listen for the sound of paper tearing when using the steaming wand on your espresso machine, and then continue for a couple of seconds longer.

Use a large spoon to hold the bubbles back while you pour the steamed milk directly on top of the espresso shot and syrup in your mug.

Use the same spoon to ladle the foam bubbles out of the pitcher and onto the top of the drink.

If you're going to be adding latte art, skip the bubbles on top and go straight to the art instead.

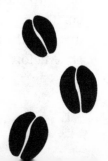

IF YOU WANT TO MAKE A FLAT WHITE INSTEAD OF A TRADITIONAL LATTE, YOU CAN FOLLOW THESE STEPS WITH A FEW MINOR CHANGES. WHEN YOU STEAM THE MILK, TRY TO GET AS FEW BUBBLES AS POSSIBLE. AND WHEN YOU POUR THE MILK INTO THE MUG OVER THE ESPRESSO, DO SO CAREFULLY AND SLOWLY SO THAT YOU CAN SEE ONLY A SINGLE WHITE DOT OF MILK ON TOP OF THE BEVERAGE. THIS IS THE SIGNATURE FLAT WHITE LOOK.

CAPPUCCINOS

Americans, and especially those who drink their coffee and espresso from chain cafes instead of locally-owned ones, tend to have the wrong idea of what a cappuccino really is. Some people believe that it is more or less the same thing as a latte, but that isn't really true. A cappuccino may be made from steamed milk and espresso like a latte, but that's where the similarities end. One of the biggest differences is the weight of the drink; if you pick up a latte and a cappuccino in the same size cup, the cappuccino should be significantly lighter in weight.

Traditionally, cappuccinos are truly decadent drinks that are made with either whole milk or heavy cream. However, you can make yours with any type of milk you prefer, so you don't have to feel limited by this unless you just want to have a more authentic experience. The key to a true cappuccino is to have plenty of milk foam, which is what sets it apart from any other espresso-based beverage. You are looking to create micro-foam on top of the steamed milk, which will sit lightly on top of the liquid in your cup and give you a frothy, delicious experience.

Cappuccinos are made with a double shot base, so you'll need to pull two shots of espresso to get started on this drink. If you have a smaller espresso machine that can only manage one shot at a time, just pull them back to back as quickly as you can so they do not go stale before you're able to enjoy them.

Pour the double shot of espresso into an appropriately sized mug.

Place four ounces of milk in your steaming pitcher and prepare your steaming wand. Place the steaming wand into the milk just a little away from the bottom of the pitcher and begin steaming.

Almost immediately, pull the wand back to just under the surface of the milk and steam until you have enough foam to double the milk in the pitcher. You are looking for smaller microbubbles in this foam, but if you have a few larger bubbles that's okay.

Use a spoon to gently scoop all the foam off the top of the milk and place it in the cup on top of the double shot. It should be light enough to sit on top of the drink and should not collapse immediately.

For a true, traditional cappuccino, you will not need to add any additional milk. The foam will begin to melt somewhat into the espresso and will create the perfect balance.

A real cappuccino also does not include any sugar or flavor. Of course, you can add flavor to the espresso shots if you want to, but it won't be a traditional take on the drink if you do so. If you choose to add flavor, use liquid syrup or liquid cane sugar and add a small amount to the double espresso shot before you spoon on the steamed milk.

MACCHIATOS

A somewhat lesser-known but still quite popular take on espresso is the macchiato. Like the cappuccino, the American take on this classic is very different from the original. A true Italian espresso macchiato is made with either one or two shots of espresso topped with a small amount of steamed milk. There's nothing else added to it, and sweetening it is not considered an option if you're making a traditional version of the drink. This is a good choice for anyone who enjoys very bold and somewhat bitter espresso drinks and needs a quick pick-me-up with a little caffeine. Another name for this drink is a caffe macchiato.

The American version of a macchiato is very different. This twist on the classic basically flips the traditional drink upside-down and changes the layering. It's also considered fine and even recommended to sweeten or flavor an American-style macchiato. Since the two versions are so vastly different from each other, we will give you instructions for how to make both styles of macchiato below. This way, you'll be able to try both for yourself and see which one you prefer—and how much of an espresso purist you may really be.

TO MAKE A TRADITIONAL ESPRESSO MACCHIATO:

» Pull one or two shots of espresso into a small espresso mug or cup. Some recommend using affogato, or short, espresso shots to make the coffee naturally sweeter, but others do not. This choice is up to you.

» Steam a small amount of milk in your steaming pitcher. Use 2% or whole milk for a traditional option or stick to other favorites if you prefer.

» Spoon a small amount of milk onto the espresso shots in your cup. Aim for a two-to-one ratio with more espresso than milk. Do not sweeten or flavor.

TO MAKE AN AMERICAN MACCHIATO:

» Begin by pulling two shots of espresso and setting them aside.

» Steam enough milk to fill your cup or mug of choice. Aim for a good amount of foam on top, but don't go all the way to cappuccino levels of foam.

» If you're going to sweeten or flavor the drink, put the syrup or sweetener into the bottom of your mug first.

» Pour the milk and foam into the mug.

» Carefully pour both shots of espresso on top of the milk foam. It will not be visible right on top, but you will see two "dots" of espresso where you poured it in. This is the look you're going for.

How to Make Latte Art

Have you ever been to a café where the barista has drawn a

perfect heart, butterfly, or pair of wings in your coffee? Have you ever seen intricate latte art designs in photos online? If you've ever noticed latte art and caught yourself wishing you knew how to do it? Don't worry. It's not too hard to get the hang of making latte designs, and once you understand how to put together a traditional latte the right way, you're already halfway there. In this chapter, we'll give you the tips you need to know in order to make a beautiful latte topped with art.

WHAT YOU NEED

You don't need very much to get started working on your latte art magic. As long as you have access to the right ingredients and to a machine that can pull espresso shots and create steamed milk, you'll be ready to get started diving into the creative process in no time. Take some time to practice making a latte without art first and you'll be even better prepared to make beautiful designs in no time.

Espresso. You cannot really make latte art without starting with espresso, as traditional coffee simply won't hold up to it.

Steamed milk. Ideally, you will have steamed milk from a steaming wand, but you can also make it on the stove if you have experience doing so without burning it. Whole milk, cream, and 2% make better latte art than others, but you can use any milk you prefer.

USE LARGE, WIDE MUGS. You need something big enough to hold the drink while giving you plenty of room to create and design.

TOOTHPICKS, CHOPSTICKS, OR ANYTHING ELSE SIMILARLY SHAPED. These instruments will help you gently move the milk around as needed in the cup to create the art you're looking for. Try to use wooden items so you don't disrupt the flavor of the espresso with plastic or metal.

PRACTICE. Nobody gets it right the first time, so be patient with yourself as you learn. You may need to make quite a few lattes before you get the hang of your latte art, so have some fun with it!

Remember to pour quickly enough to keep the milk moving the way it needs to, but not so fast that you splash it or the espresso.

Keep the pitcher of milk close to the top of the drink when pouring, but not so close that the pitcher scrapes the foam.

EASY DESIGNS TO TRY AT HOME

Here are a few simple latte art designs you can try for yourself. Of course, there are many more complicated styles you may want to delve into after you learn how to do these, but it's a good idea to start small and work your way up. Although latte art isn't too challenging, there is a knack to it, and it takes a little time to learn. Remember that only espresso and steamed milk can be used to make latte art.

HEART. The classic latte art design, the heart, is one of the easiest to master. Start pouring milk back and forth to make a large circle in the center of the drink. Then, pull the milk quickly forward to create a straight line that divides the heart shape at the top and makes the point at the bottom. This quick motion can be tricky, so try it until you get it right.

Another simple twist on the heart design involves making many small hearts around the edge of the cup. To do this, pour a little milk near the edge of the mug and stop as soon as you notice a white spot on top. Repeat this process several times around the perimeter of the mug. Drag a toothpick or chopstick through the dots quickly to make the divide between the heart and add the points at the bottom of each one.

LEAF. This simple design is another good choice for beginners. Pour your milk slowly from side to side in the cup, creating stripes as you work your way from the top to the bottom of the mug. At the end, divide the design with a quick pour down the middle, just like with the heart design.

FLOWER. This one is a little tougher, but it's a good intermediate latte art design. Start pouring the milk down into the drink, about an inch or so from the bottom of the cup. When you're half done with this, start moving the milk from side to side, working your way across to the opposite edge of the mug. This movement can take some practice, and it's all in your wrist. Try not to overdo it by making larger motions with your arm, and you should have better control of the milk.

HELPFUL HINTS

Getting your latte art right takes time, but there are some tips and hints you can keep in mind to make the experience go a little more smoothly. Remember the following when you find yourself struggling or just want to improve your latte drawing:

Warming up your mug first with hot water (and then pouring it out) before adding the espresso can help with your latte art designs. This will help keep the espresso and milk warm and flowing more smoothly as you pour. Additionally, it's also good for improving the overall flavor and aroma of the drink.

Choose a thicker milk, like whole milk or cream, while you're learning. You can make latte art with 2%, skim, soy, and others, but it's easier to learn with heavier milks.

Master the art of steaming milk before you try latte art. You want milk that is smooth and velvety, and you need to be able to pour it without letting the foam get into your drink. A little foam is okay, but too much will affect the way the milk pours and lays in the cup, and this will make it difficult or even impossible to make latte art.

EXPANDING YOUR HORIZONS

Now that you've explored

everything there is to know about coffee—from farming to roasting, from brewing to building drinks—it's time to go a little beyond the norm and consider some other ways you might want to use coffee and espresso in your everyday life. Whether you're looking for a new and exciting coffee drink to try, or you want to start cooking with the flavors of espresso, we've got several suggestions below to help you get started.

COFFEE-BASED DRINKS

Coffee and espresso can be more than the traditional go-to hot drinks you know and love. Consider these options to help you find a good fit for your unique coffee needs, and don't be afraid to play around a little bit with them to create something inspired and original.

ICED COFFEE. This is one of the easiest and most common twists on regular coffee. It's simple to make, since all you need to do is cool the coffee down somewhat and pour it over ice. However, it's also easy to get the proportions wrong. As the ice in the coffee melts, it will water down the drink and can actually make it taste rather unpleasant. For this reason, it's usually recommended to use strongly brewed coffee for icing, and some companies and vendors will offer specific blends intended for this purpose, too.

BLACK TIE. This coffee drink is also known as a Thai iced tea. This is a very powerful drink with a big caffeine punch. The drink is made by boiling water and steeping Thai tea mix with sugar for a few minutes. While the tea steeps, prepare a glass filled nearly all the way with ice. Add a tablespoon of condensed milk and a shot of espresso to the ice in the glass. Pour the steeped tea over the top and then finish it off with another two tablespoons of dairy—either whole milk or cream for best results. Stir until the entire drink is blended together well.

CHAI TEA LATTE. A chai tea latte can be one of many things, but they are all very similar. In some instances, people use the phrase "chai latte" to refer to a drink that is made from steeping chai tea in steamed milk, with no coffee involved at all. However, technically speaking, this drink should be made with a shot of regular brewed coffee stirred in at the end to give it a distinct spicy, bitter flavor. Some cafés will use a shot of espresso instead of brewed coffee instead, and this is referred to as a "dirty chai."

RED EYE. This is another strong pick-me-up kind of drink, so named for its high caffeine content and the implication that it will prepare you for a red-eye shift or flight. This drink is simple, but it has a kick. It's made with a cup of brewed coffee—usually dark roast, but any roast is fine—with a shot of espresso poured in at the end. It's up to the drinker to determine whether or not it needs sugar or milk.

IRISH COFFEE. A true Irish coffee is a little bit more than just coffee and alcohol put together, but this is the general idea. To make an Irish coffee, first heat up a mug with hot water and then empty it out. Pour in enough hot, freshly brewed coffee to fill about three-quarters of the mug. Stir in a tablespoon of brown sugar and then add a jigger of Irish whiskey, stirring gently to disperse it throughout the drink. Finally, top it off by gently pouring heavy cream into the drink.

BLENDED COFFEE/FRAPPÉ. This type of drink may not appeal very much to a coffee purist, but the truth is that blended cold coffee beverages are very popular. These drinks are usually made by putting milk, coffee or espresso, ice, and flavorings into a blender and letting it work its magic. They have a consistency sort of like a milkshake, but not exactly. Depending on the preference of the person drinking it, these beverages can be changed and altered in all sorts of ways.

COFFEE-BASED DESSERTS

When you love the taste of coffee and can't get enough of it, you might want to try making some desserts with coffee and espresso as an ingredient, too. Try the options below for some good starters, and then expand even further to find more interesting ways to incorporate coffee into your after dinner treats.

TIRAMISU. This is the classic coffee dessert, and you may have tried it before. This decadent treat is made from ladyfingers (which are similar to sponge cake) that are soaked in coffee to give them a distinct flavor. These coffee cakes are layered between sweetened mascarpone cheese and the whole concoction is topped off with cocoa shavings. This is a very well-known and beloved dessert that has several variations, and you can easily tweak it, redesign it, and make it your own.

ESPRESSO BROWNIES. Love the taste of brownies and want to take them up a notch? Consider adding some espresso to the mix! Espresso brownies can be a delicious, rich, and indulgent way to get your coffee and chocolate fix at the same time. It's easy to change the recipe for most brownies to incorporate espresso, but you can also find specific recipes intended for this purpose as well.

MOCHA TRUFFLES. Mocha truffles are chocolate truffles that have either espresso or coffee as an ingredient. Using a coffee element for your truffle filling can give the candies a distinct flavor and aroma that adds layers of interest to the dessert, rather than relying solely on chocolate.

COFFEE MOUSSE. Last but not least, consider making a coffee mousse if you want something light and airy but still packed with coffee taste. You can make a coffee mousse by sprinkling gelatin over cold coffee and folding whipped cream and beaten egg whites into it. This is the same concept as making other types of mousse, but it utilizes coffee as the liquid component.

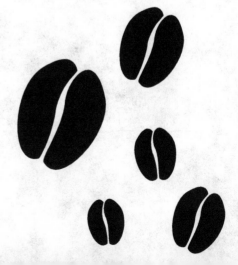

CONCLUSION

The world of coffee is a vibrant and exciting one. Understanding the whole coffee experience can help you enjoy the drink in ways you never have before. Knowing how to buy and choose coffee, as well as where it comes from and what it takes to grow it, may improve your ability to make better purchasing decisions. And of course, learning how to make different drinks—from roasting to grinding to brewing right in your own home—can allow you to create beverages you'll want to sip over and over again. Now that you have expanded your knowledge of this classic drink, you can share your coffee passion with your family and friends!

FREE BONUS:

10 FREE RECIPES FOR DELICIOUS COFFEE DRINKS YOU CAN MAKE AT HOME

GO TO HTTP://TINYURL.COM/Y5X5T4FN
TO DOWNLOAD YOUR FREE RECIPE BOOK

Download The Audio Version Of This Book Free!

CPSIA information can be obtained
at www.ICGtesting.com
Printed in the USA
BVHW071926280821
615438BV00003B/394